BEAVERS

Beaver Magic for Kids

To all kids who love beavers, and to Dr. Richard Coles,
a grown-up who loves beavers.

— Patricia Corrigan

For a free catalog describing Gareth Stevens Publishing's list of high-quality books, call 1-800-542-2595 (USA) or 1-800-461-9120 (Canada).
Gareth Stevens Publishing's Fax: 414-225-0377.
See our catalog, too, on the World Wide Web: http://gsinc.com

Library of Congress Cataloging-in-Publication Data available upon request from the publisher.
Fax: (414) 225-0377 for the attention of the Publishing Records Department.

ISBN 0-8368-1629-3

First published in this edition in
North America in 1996 by
Gareth Stevens Publishing
1555 North RiverCenter Drive, Suite 201
Milwaukee, Wisconsin 53212 USA

Based on the book *Beavers for Kids*, text © 1996 by Patricia Corrigan, with illustrations by John F. McGee. First published in the United States in 1996 by NorthWord Press, Inc., Minocqua, Wisconsin. End matter © 1996 by Gareth Stevens, Inc.

Photographs © 1996: Mike Barlow/Dembinsky Photo Associates, Cover; Tom & Pat Leeson, 7, 8, 15, 16-17, 26, 28-29; Jen & Des Bartlett/Bruce Coleman, Inc., 18-19, 21; Jonathan T. Wright/Bruce Coleman, Inc., 27; Skip Moody/Dembinsky Photo Associates, 31; Dominique Braud/Dembinsky Photo Associates, 33; Jim Brandenburg/Minden Pictures, 40; F-Stock, Inc., 44-45; Leonard Lee Rue III, 46; Len Rue, Jr., 3, 10-11, 36, 39, Back Cover.

Printed in the United States of America

1 2 3 4 5 6 7 8 9 99 98 97 96

by Patricia Corrigan

BEAVERS

Beaver Magic for Kids

Gareth Stevens Publishing
MILWAUKEE

I like to walk in the woods near my house. It is so quiet, you can hear everything that moves. And there's always something new to see. My name is Antonio and I'm 11.

One day, on a hike in the woods, I noticed right away that something was different about my favorite stream. A big, dark animal was swimming in the water up ahead. At first I couldn't tell exactly what it was. I didn't want to scare the animal away. I tiptoed over to the edge of the bank for a closer look and sat down.

I guess I did scare it, because it disappeared. I kept watching the spot where I first saw it. All of a sudden, it popped up again, closer to me than before.

It was a beaver!

At first, I thought it had a really high back. So I squinted to see better. What I saw was two beavers—an adult beaver and a baby beaver.

Beavers are some of nature's best architects and engineers. Some people appreciate beavers, because the dams they build create habitats for other creatures. Sometimes, a dam stops a bank from washing away, or saves a stream that is drying up.

Other people say beavers are destructive, because they cut down too many trees. I believe that beavers only take what they need.

I watched the beavers swim and dive until finally they disappeared again. Then I headed back to the house because it was starting to get dark. I was lucky to see those beavers. Usually, people see only evidence of beavers—signs that they live nearby.

Part of the reason people don't often see beavers is because they are nocturnal (that's pronounced NOK-TUR-NUL), which means they rest during the day and come out mostly at night.

Beavers are rodents, and they are related to squir-rels and mice—but they are much bigger. Beavers have small heads, small eyes and small ears. Their bodies aren't so small, though. Adult beavers grow to be about 4 1/2 feet in length and weigh between 40 and 60 pounds. The biggest beaver on record weighed 108 pounds!

Of course, that was the biggest beaver in modern times. About 35 million years ago, huge prehistoric beavers lived on Earth. They were about 10 feet long, with 30-inch-long tails. Those beavers weighed as much as 700 pounds.

Today, beavers can be found in almost every state and throughout most of Canada. They live to be 7 to 10 years old in the wild. Most beavers are brown, but not just plain old brown. Their fur can be dark brown, reddish brown, and light brown.

Beaver fur is like a waterproof jacket. On top are long, silky "guard" hairs that protect the dense and woolly fur underneath. In a special gland near the base of the tail, beavers carry their own supply of oil. They use that oil to keep their fur smooth, and as a water repellent to keep themselves dry.

Beavers also make a scent called castoreum (KAS-TOR-EE-UM) that they use to mark their territory. The scent serves as a warning that some beavers already live in the area, and other beavers should look elsewhere to build a home.

Even if you've never seen a beaver, you probably know about its tail. Flat and shaped like a paddle, a beaver's tail is about 3/4 inch thick. The tail grows up to 12 inches long and is 6 to 8 inches wide. Unlike the rest of the furry beaver, the tail is covered in scales, like a snake or a fish.

When they are in the water, beavers use their tails like boat rudders, for steering. They also slap their tails on the water's surface, just as whales do, making a loud noise and a great splash with every slap. I would really like to hear that someday!

Scientists who study animals are called zoologists (ZO-OL-O-JISTS). Some of them think beavers slap their tails to warn each other of possible danger. Or maybe they are warning other animals (or people) to keep away from beaver territory. Beavers have been observed slapping their tails at birds, deer, other beavers, and even a 1,000-pound moose.

Because of their scaly tails, beavers once were thought to be fish. But beavers are air-breathing, warm-blooded mammals, just like people. Unlike most people, though, beavers spend a lot of time in the water. Beavers swim about 2 miles per hour, and can swim continuously underwater for about half a mile. That's a lot faster and farther than I can swim!

Beavers paddle with their strong hind feet when they swim, keeping their front feet curled close to their chests. I don't think I could swim with my arms curled in like that.

Their ears and noses have special valves that close underwater. Transparent membranes, sort of like the goggles I wear in the water, protect their eyes as they swim. Special furry patches inside their mouths close to prevent beavers from swallowing water when they carry branches or eat underwater.

Baby beavers, like the one I saw, are called kits. They are born late in the spring. Usually, a litter consists of four kits, weighing less than a pound each. A kit is about 8 or 9 inches long and is born with a baby-sized 3 1/2-inch-long tail.

When they are born, kits are covered in fur. The little ones make noises that sound like high-pitched squeals. Adult beavers make mumbling sounds, soft nasal sounds, and lower-pitched squeals.

Kits are also born with another very special feature. In fact, I think it's what makes a beaver a beaver: big front teeth.

Every beaver has four incisors (IN-SIZE-ORS). Two are on the bottom and two are on the top. These teeth can be up to 2 inches long. That's about eight times longer than my teeth! The beaver's sharp, strong teeth can cut through trees very quickly. Its other teeth, in the back, are used for grinding food.

Beaver incisors are interesting to see. The hard coating on the front—called enamel—is very unusual. It's bright orange!

I couldn't wait to get back to the stream the next day. I looked around the area where I had seen the beavers the day before. I found a dam that they had built with sticks of different sizes, stones, and mud. The dam held back some of the water, which made part of the stream deeper. Beavers build dams in streams, rivers, marshes, and small lakes. Some big dams have measured as much as 12 feet high and 600 feet long. That's as long as two football fields!

I noticed that there were some holes in the dam. The heavy spring rains probably had damaged it. The beavers would have to make repairs, and that means they would have to cut down some trees.

Here is how a beaver cuts down a tree: With its tail extended for balance, the beaver stands on its hind feet and gnaws at the bark with its sharp incisors. The beaver cuts two deep notches, then strips off the bark and gnaws through the wood.

Eventually, the tree falls. The beaver is careful to stay out of the way of the falling tree. Trees that grow on the edge of the river bank often grow out over the water, so they fall right in. Then, the beaver goes into the water and cuts the branches into small pieces.

When a tree falls on land, the beaver bites off the branches and drags them toward the water. Sometimes, beavers dig canals on the land next to ponds and streams. After the canals fill with water, the beavers float the large limbs and tree trunks to their dams.

Some scientists say beavers are intelligent. There have been reports of people trying to outsmart beavers by wrapping wire netting around the bottoms of some trees so the beavers couldn't cut them down. But the beavers stacked up branches next to those trees like a ladder, climbed up on top of the stack and cut down the trees just above the netting.

Usually, beavers work alone when cutting trees. But sometimes beaver families, called colonies, work together on big projects. For example, a beaver colony in British Columbia, Canada, cut down a cottonwood tree over 6 feet wide and 110 feet high!

A colony is made up of an adult male, an adult female, and their youngest offspring. Sometimes a few beavers that were born to them the previous year also live with the colony. But older offspring usually move on to other sites, to build dams and start families of their own.

Most beavers get along well with their family members. That's lucky, because they spend a lot of time living together in close quarters. When beavers argue, they hiss and lunge at each other. But they rarely strike out with their strong claws or bite with their sharp teeth.

Many beavers live in beaver lodges. A lodge is a home built of tree branches and limbs. It is plastered together with mud and anchored to the shore.

Each beaver lodge has one big room, about 4 feet wide and 3 feet high. The room has a floor above the water covered with soft grasses. The animals sleep there, and take refuge during harsh winters. Each lodge has secret tunnels, called plunge holes, with entrances underwater. That way, beavers can come and go without being seen.

The beavers I saw didn't have a lodge. The bank was too high and the stream often flooded. So, they burrowed into the bank instead of building a lodge on the water.

Bank dens are built above the water line, so the beavers have a dry place to sleep. The dens are smaller than lodges, but they also have tunnels that lead directly into the water.

Those tunnels can be used to escape enemies. Some common beaver enemies include coyotes, bobcats, lynx, otters, minks, wolverines, and bears. But people are the main enemy of beavers. The animals lose their homes and their sources of food when marshes are drained or land is cleared to build more houses for people. And some beavers die when the water where they live is polluted by chemicals.

In colonial times, people wanted hats, coats, and purses made from the beaver's thick fur. The beavers were nearly wiped out.

At that time, beavers may have been diurnal (DI-YER-NUL). That means they were active during the day, and asleep at night. Some zoologists say the reason beavers now are active at night is because they learned they could survive longer if they stayed out of sight during the day.

Many people thought it was important to save beavers from extinction. They spoke with government officials, and laws were made to protect beavers. They also made a plan to move the few remaining beavers to areas where they would thrive.

It worked. Today, there are lots of beavers—like the ones near my favorite stream.

When I walked back to the stream a couple days later, I saw some fallen trees on the opposite bank. I used to think beavers used all the wood they cut down to build their dams or the lodges they live in, but they also eat some of it.

Beavers love bark best. They also find spring leaves on trees very tasty. They'll eat cottonwood, willow, oak, aspen, beech, alder, hickory, and birch trees, just to name a few. They also eat water plants and small shrubs they find on land. Beavers eat about 2 pounds of food every day.

In some parts of the country, where the winters are long and cold, beavers stash tree limbs underwater near their lodges or dens, so they don't have to go far to find food. When they are hungry, beavers leave their home and swim under the ice. They breathe air trapped between the top of the water and the ice. Sometimes, beavers have to break a hole through the ice to breathe better.

Beavers spend lots of time grooming themselves—as much as an hour a day. When it's time to get cleaned up, the beaver climbs out of the water and sits down on its tail. Using all four paws, the beaver rubs its entire body, clearing away any leaves, twigs, mud, or pond scum that may be stuck to its fur. They also use their paws like combs to get rid of tangles!

I decided to keep walking down the stream, to see if I could find more signs of beavers. Was I glad I did! I found another small dam and a den. And I saw footprints that I know belonged to a beaver.

I could tell this because a beaver's front and back feet don't match. The front paws have five "fingers," like raccoons and people have. Each finger has a sharp claw, used for digging and holding food. Beavers eat twigs just the way we eat corn on the cob—they hold it and turn it, nibbling as they go.

Their hind feet resemble a duck's feet. They are webbed—all five toes are connected with skin. Each hind foot has two claws.

When I saw the foot-
prints in the sand, I fol-
lowed them downstream
for awhile. Then I sat on
the bank to rest. Suddenly,
I heard splashing. It was
two beavers!

They rolled over and
over in the water. They
dived. They turned somer-
saults. They popped up
and darted back down into
the water. They glided up
and over each others'
backs. They even played
what looked like a game of
tag. They seemed to be
having lots of fun.

After seeing the beavers and getting to watch so many of their activities, I plan on doing a lot more hiking.

After all, you never know what you might discover on a walk through the woods.

GLOSSARY

Castoreum: The scent produced by a beaver that is used to mark territory (page 12).

Colony: A family group of animals. A beaver colony usually consists of an adult male and female with their youngest offspring (page 30).

Habitat: The place where an animal or plant lives in the wild (page 6).

Incisor: A tooth adapted for cutting (page 22).

Kits: The young of some fur-bearing animals, including beavers (page 21).

Mammal: A warm-blooded vertebrate with some hair on its body. Mammals produce milk to feed their young (page 19).

Plunge hole: A secret tunnel in a beaver lodge that has an underwater entrance (page 34).

Zoologist: A scientist who studies animals (page 16).

ADULT-CHILD INTERACTION QUESTIONS

These are questions designed to encourage young readers to participate in further study and discussion of beavers.

1. How long can a beaver stay under the water?
2. Do beavers eat only vegetation?
3. How do beavers build their lodges?
4. Do people still hunt and trap beavers?
5. Which states in the United States do not have beavers?
6. Do other kinds of animals have oil-producing glands for waterproofing?
7. How long does it take a beaver to cut down a tree?

MORE BOOKS TO READ

The Beaver by Anne Marie Dalmais (Rourke)
Beaver by Emilie U. Lepthien (Childrens Press)
The Beaver by Hope Ryden (Putnam)
The Beaver Pond by Alvin R. Tresselt (Lothrop, Lee & Shepard)
Busy Beaver by Lydia Dabeovich (Dutton)

VIDEOS

The Beaver (Phoenix/BFA)
A Beaver Pond (National Geographic Society)